LIVING IN... INDIA

by Chloe Perkins
illustrated by Tom Woolley

READY-TO-READ

SIMON SPOTLIGHT

An imprint of Simon & Schuster Children's Publishing Division • New York   London   Toronto   Sydney   New Delhi • 1230 Avenue of the Americas, New York, New York 10020 • This Simon Spotlight edition October 2016 • Text copyright © 2016 by Simon & Schuster, Inc. Illustrations copyright © 2016 by Tom Woolley • All rights reserved, including the right of reproduction in whole or in part in any form. SIMON SPOTLIGHT, READY-TO-READ, and colophon are registered trademarks of Simon & Schuster, Inc. For information about special discounts for bulk purchases, please contact Simon & Schuster Special Sales at 1-866-506-1949 or business@simonandschuster.com. Manufactured in the United States of America 0721 LAK   6 8 10 9 7
Library of Congress Cataloging-in-Publication Data
Names: Perkins, Chloe, author. | Woolley, Tom, 1981- illustrator. Title: Living in . . . India / by Chloe Perkins ; illustrated by Tom Woolley. Other titles: India | Description: New York : Simon & Schuster, [2016] | Series: Living in . . . series | "Ready-to-Read, Simon Spotlight." | Audience: Grades K-3.? Identifiers: LCCN 2015046309 | ISBN 9781481470896 (trade paper) | ISBN 9781481470902 (hardcover) | ISBN 9781481470919 (eBook) Subjects: LCSH: India—Juvenile literature. Classification: LCC DS407 .P42 2016 | DDC 954—dc23   LC record available at http://lccn.loc.gov/2015046309

GLOSSARY

Cricket: a popular game in India that is similar to baseball

Crop: a plant or something that comes from a plant, such as fruits or vegetables

Flatbread: a kind of bread that is flat and thin

Hobby class: lessons that children take in their spare time in subjects, such as dance, sports, or cooking

Imprison: to put someone in jail

Independence: being free from outside control

Movement: a series of actions that people take to bring about changes in their government

Musical: a play or movie in which much of the story is told through song

Plateau: a flat area of land that is raised higher than the land around it

Region: a place with certain geographic features that make it different from the surrounding area

Resource: a supply of items that is valuable, useful, or important

Souvenir: an item brought back from a place someone visited

Taxes: money that people pay to their government for public services, such as building roads or keeping a military

Temple: a building used to practice one's religion

Traditional: a way of doing something that has been passed down within a group for a long time

NOTE TO READERS: Some of these words may have more than one definition. The definitions above are how these words are used in this book.

Namaskār! (say: nah-mus-KAR) That means "hi" in Marathi (say: muh-RAH-tee). My name is Nisha, and I live in India. India is a country in Asia where more than one billion people live . . . including me!

India is made up of twenty-nine states. People in different states often speak different languages. This is because India is very big. It is the seventh-largest country in the world. More than seven hundred languages are spoken in India.

India is split into four
main geographic regions.
The north of India is
part of the Himalayan
mountain range.
To the south is the
Deccan Plateau, which
has many hills and rivers.

The region above the plateau is large and flat and is great for growing crops because many rivers run through it. This area has lots of farms. The last region, to the west, is covered in deserts.

India has many big, bustling cities. One of the biggest is Mumbai (say: MUM-bye). In Mumbai you'll find "Bollywood" where a lot of movies in India are made. India makes the most movies in the world! Many of them are musicals.

The biggest city in India is Delhi (say: DELL-ee). Within Delhi is our capital, New Delhi, which is home to many beautiful temples and museums. You can find the Lotus Temple there. It is one of the most famous temples in India!

NEW DELHI

BENGALURU

Bengaluru (BEN-guh-loo-roo)
is known as the Garden City.
It is filled with blooming
trees, big parks, and lakes.
Kolkata has been home to many
of India's great thinkers, artists,
writers, and architects over the years.

KOLKATA

I live near Mumbai
in a city called Pune (say: POO-nay)
with my mom, dad,
and two sisters.
I have one older sister
and one younger sister.

My dad is an airline pilot. He flies people to places all around the world. My mom works for a real estate company. She helps people buy homes and apartments.

Each morning I wake up and get dressed. There are many different kinds of clothes in India, like the sari (say: SAH-ree) and the *kurti* (say: KOOR-tee). I wear saris to fancy events like weddings. A sari is a long cloth that you wrap around yourself.

SARI

At home I often wear shorts,
but at school I wear a uniform.
My older sister usually
wears a kurti. A kurti is a long
shirt that you wear with pants.

KURTI

After I get dressed, I have
breakfast with my mom
and sisters. I usually eat
idli (say: ID-lee), which are
rice cakes. I dip the idli in a
vegetable stew called
sambar (say: SAHM-bahr).

Time for school! I take
an auto rickshaw to school.
An auto rickshaw is a three-wheeled
car. I live ten minutes from
school. The auto rickshaw
picks up other students
along the way.

School starts really early, at 7:10 a.m. At my school there are two shifts, one in the morning and one in the afternoon. Different students attend each shift. We have two shifts because there are too many students to have in school at the same time.

There are fifty-six students
in my class. Each day we
study math, science, history,
Marathi—which is the
language of our state—
and either art, music, or gym.

Our first subject is math.
We are learning about
subtraction.
After our math lesson
we practice reading
in English and Marathi.

In the big cities in India
most students learn English.
It is important to learn
English because many
medicine labels,
menus, and signs
in India are printed
in English.

At ten o'clock we stop
for our snack break.
Today we are having
flatbread with sabzi (say: SUHB-zee).
Sabzi is a dish made from
cooked vegetables.
Once we finish our snack,
we start our history lesson.

We are learning about when the British ruled India from 1858 to 1947. Britain wanted to control India because our country had valuable spices, rice, cotton, tea, and gems. India's resources made Britain very rich.

RICE

The British built factories and
railroads all over India to make
and move more goods. But many
Indian people were unhappy.
Britain made Indians work for
little money and fight in their wars.
During food shortages in India,
Britain did little to help.

As time passed, people wanted the British to leave.
A man named Mohandas Gandhi (say: moh-HUHN-dahs GAHN-dee) began a movement to end British rule in 1919. Gandhi told people to stop attending British schools and to stop working for the British.

Gandhi was imprisoned a few times, including once right here in Pune! But that didn't stop him.
He told the people to make their own food, clothes, and other goods. This way the British couldn't make money from taxes on the goods that Indian people bought.

It took many years,
but Gandhi's ideas worked.
In 1945 the British began
talking to Gandhi and
other leaders about
Indian independence.
And in 1947 Britain at last gave
power back to the Indian people!

After science and gym class
it's noon, and school is over!
I take the auto rickshaw home.
I play cricket with my
sisters and our friends.
Cricket is a very popular
sport in India.

At six o'clock I have my
hobby class. Hobby classes are
outside of school, and you can
learn all kinds of subjects.
My big sister learns a
traditional Indian dance. My
little sister learns piano. I get
to learn speed roller-skating!

When we get home, my sisters and I discuss Diwali (say: dih-WAH-lee). Diwali is a Hindu festival celebrated for five days in October or November and marks the new year in India.

On the first day we clean the house.

We light clay lamps, which represent our inner light, on the second day.

On the third day we eat yummy food and watch fireworks.

We exchange gifts on the fourth day.

And on the fifth day we have a big meal with our uncles.

After we talk about Diwali,
we eat dinner. Tonight we
are having vegetable curry.
Curry is a spicy sauce that
you eat over rice. After dinner
our dad gets home from
his latest trip. He brought
my sisters and me souvenirs!

My dad brings me back
souvenirs from all his trips.
I have things from China and
Iceland and the United States, too!
One day I want to visit all
of these places, just like my dad.
Would you like to visit
India someday?

ALL ABOUT
INDIA!

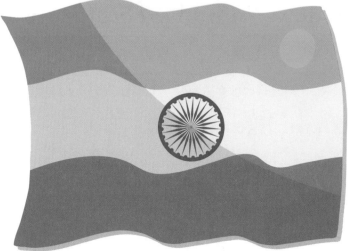

NAME: Republic of India (or India for short!)

POPULATION: 1.25 billion

CAPITAL: New Delhi

LANGUAGE: 41 percent of people speak Hindi, but some 780 languages are spoken in India! The most popular are Bengali, Telugu, Nisha's native Marathi, Tamil, Urdu, and English.

TOTAL AREA: 1,269,219 square miles

GOVERNMENT: federal parliamentary republic

CURRENCY: rupee

FUN FACT: Did you notice the people flying kites in this book? India celebrates its independence each year on August 15 with ceremonies, speeches, and kite-flying! The kites symbolize freedom.

FLAG: Three equal-size horizontal stripes of saffron (orange), white, and green. The symbol at the center is a blue chakra, or twenty-four-spoked wheel, which symbolizes life and death.